With the words that God has given me.

I present my first written birth.

A
Lift
In
Life

Jinia M.

{I met with an accident in 2015 which hurt me in more than one place. And I became completely homebound and almost lost my physical strength. It was then that I joined yoga with my mom's advice and tried hard to recover. But it took one and a half years to regain my body strength. Time was very tough for me and my family. But after every tough thing, good things happen. In January 2019, I started writing without knowing what I was writing. It was April 2019 that I decided to publish my first book of poetry, " A Lift In Life, with the words that God has given me}

With the words that God
has given me
i share with you
to help you
when you will be crossing
the tunnel of
shadows and darkness.

With love,

Jinia M.

First print 2019
Reprint 2021

Paperback ISBN - 978-93-5426-205-0
E-book ISBN – 978-93-5437-008-3

Illustration and design by Jinia M
Cover illustration and design by Jinia M

This book is for all those

whose tears

fall in silence

"May you find you in You."

Contents

Wordsinpen

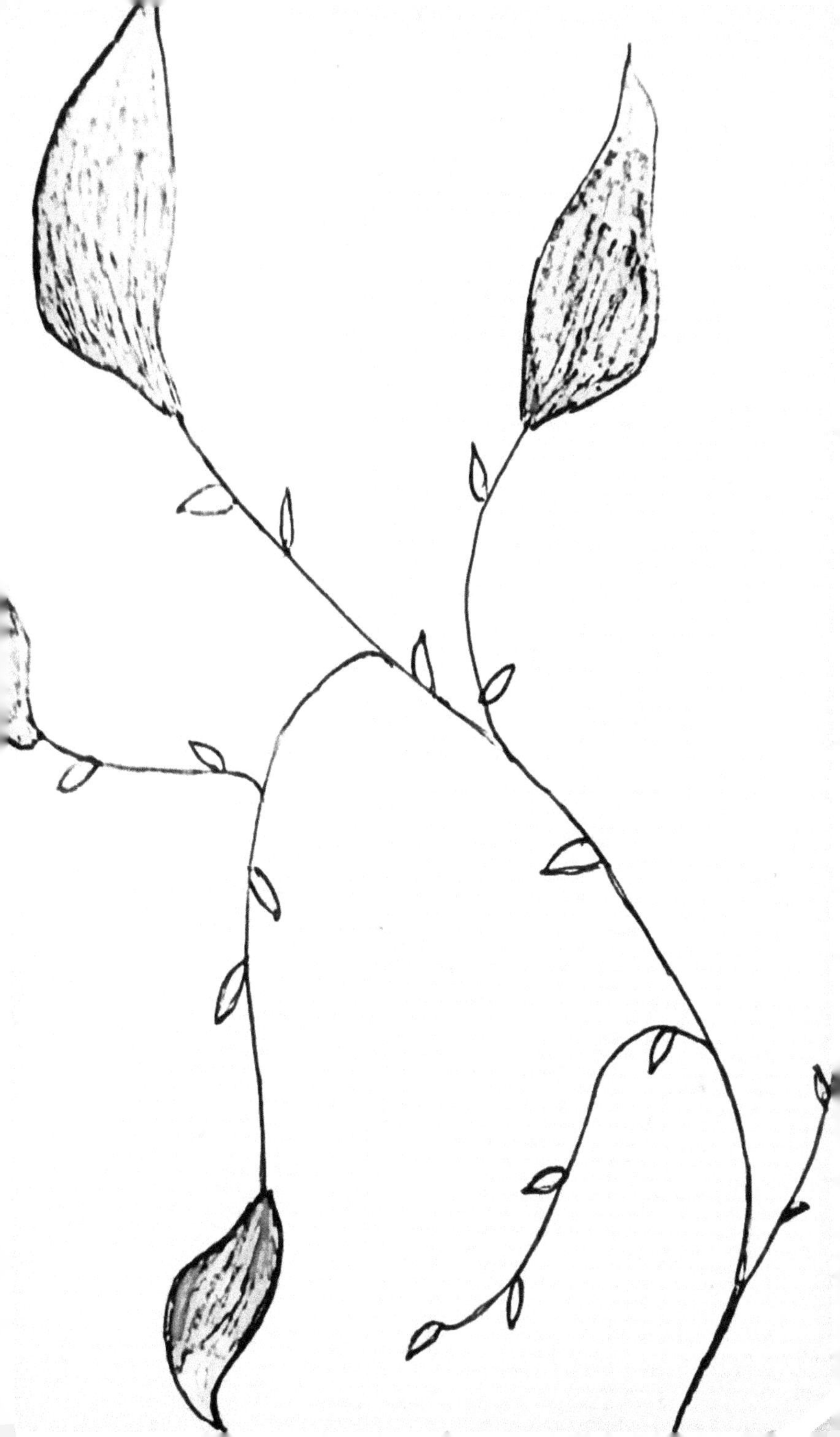

Introduction

I realise something from my daily chores that it is of no use to look back and feel sad. It is never going to be the same thing anymore. Nothing happens twice like before. Everything changes; I too have changed. No more am I the previous person. Both physically and mentally, we keep on changing. And the change has occurred to me as well. Now that I cannot be the person I was, I am a new me. I only carry faith and let me carry it for my coming days as well. A Prayer, so that I can be brave when things will happen the way I have never thought they would. The new surprises and the tragedy will be coming, but I must secure my heart and mind. I only want courage from nature, as it has in abundance. The courage will guard me against every fall I will face.

Courage will help me to rise again. Life always falls and rises. The courage will encourage me to take the next step with confidence. Courage will always lend me power when I am weak in body and mind. The courage will give me the empowerment to rule my own life by my rules of existence. I must take this opportunity to give all credit to the Universe, the Supreme Power; until now, it has been kind to me. I want that kindness to stay with me forever to help me grow in every way. Let it make me strong enough with time to accept the changes that will be coming in my life. Let it make me more graceful. In return, I promise I will remain grateful as always for this brilliant life journey. To, cherish and flourish more in the coming days as well, fulfilling all my responsibilities for my family and myself.

The positive vibes

I want
positivity
everywhere.

Days

The two days I count.
one is past
another is present.
it is our wish to dig into the past
or to open up the present.
and with faith and courage
work
for more presents.

Life

Life is a mystery,
which unfolds itself slowly
with time
the coming unknown days open up
slowly like the petals of
a rose.
a rose is as if the life,
which is, consists
of both soft
and the thorny touch;
you have to accept both in
a favourable time.
maybe sometimes,
you do not expect
something good to happen
but it suddenly happens,
you name it
a miracle.

life is always uncertain,
uncertain like seasons,
uncertain like love,
uncertain like feelings.
nothing stays
permanently

you know your past;
you can be there at any time
travelling through
your memory lane
there are good, bad,
exciting, loving and
learning memories.
You cannot stay there forever
it's past
that time is gone
it does not exist anymore.

Past life is your experiences;
past life is your journey
of various natures
to make you grow,
to make you learn
and
to unleash confidence.

All that happens in your life
transform you
to become the
person
with whom you
live today.

Second step

Life is always about the next step.
Life is always about the second step.
We are always stepping into the future.
With every moment, every second.
With every thought, with every mistake.
With every loss, with every pain.
With every opportunity, with every gain.

After every pause,
there can be motion.
after every motion,
there can be a pause.
but life keeps on moving
nothing stops life from moving
the universe never reverses
any of its laws for anyone
and neither for itself
the laws state
only future will remain
for every life.
nothing will exist
except-memories.

fall in love with
every new chance,
life is giving you
fall in love with faith;
fall in love with the dawn,
it is the beginning
of a new day,
a new dream
    with every new thought,
    a new chapter begins.

Hope

hope is positivity
hope is faith
hope is that 'word'
that makes you brave
hope brings possibilities
to tie in with new opportunities
hope brings love,
for you to grow
more in your path
hold it tight
with all your heart
it can make your journey
pleasant and
bright.

Being Fearless

once upon a time, i had a fear
that blew my mind
and my ear
through my veins to my heart
made me paralysed
my entire part,
i fought with faith
i fought with guts
to remove the avalanche
from my
path.
and i succeeded at last
to clear it from my life
from my path
from the depth of my heart
it just vanishes from my
heart.

– *believe*

Bold

the bold is honest.
the beauty is pure.
a person who is both
is not terrified for long,
doors are all slam
the miserable life
but the intensity
within remains pure,
for there are doors
to discover
and just let everything
go
feel the feel achieve the feel
for that feel,
everything is possible.

Humans

"Humanity is priceless
neither i can buy it nor
i can expect it
from others
when i see it in anyone,
i simply enjoy it
i observe it
as the creator's creation
with a new vision. "

Suffering

I know you are suffering,
I know you have suffered,
I know those people whom you trusted
a lot have cheated upon you,
I know others have submerged you,
I know that you do not have the
respect that you deserve,
I know you have struggled hard
to fill that empty part
of your life and your heart,
I know that you feel despair
when you see no clues,
I know you suffered that deep-cut
wound
in your heart that wound had torn you
apart
and outside your giving smile is fake,

I know you want to share
your feelings and your fears.
I know you want to open your heart
to speak that unspoken verse.
I know that you never wanted to fall
like this ever before.
I know you want to be happy
forever.
I know you want to get up and
show the world,
that your life also has worth.

you live and you also have
existence in this world
you are tired and
you are exhausted
even though you have given
everything
from the core of your heart
you seem not happy with what you did
for yourself and
for the person who does not deserve it,
no one has understood you
no one has tried
your soul is screaming
and it does not want to survive
there is no one to hear you;

but you do,
yes, you can hear your voice
the time has arrived now that
you must learn
your self and your self-happiness
you need to know that you are special
you need to know that you are also a
creator's creation,
like the stars and the moon in the sky
your life on earth also vibes,
you need to know how far
your journey is written
you must try to make yourself 'worth"
you must not give up
what you do not have
realise what you have
and you can hope for.

you must not neglect yourself
your capabilities,
your skills, and your dreams.

the dream, which was there
with you in your heart,
is still attached to your soul
the dream, which can be your identity,
which can give you the name
in the mob.

to give yourself that happiness
that peace you deserve
make yourself believe that you are
valuable.

wake up and take a step ahead
to make your road
to make your journey
where no one can dominate you,
where no one can hurt you
that the world will be created
only by you.

be proud of yourself by accepting the
way you are
stop regretting what you did not
get,

allow yourself to burn for all the
happiness
which once you wished for
yourself.

Keep trying
and
Keep moving

Essence

The essence of the Universe has three words
The **patience,**
The **faith** and
The **journey**.
For
The
Unknown
"Destiny".

Universe

What you give to the Universe,
Universe returns it to you with
interest.
Giving is receiving!
If you want love, give love!
If you want a smile, give a smile!
If you want respect, give respect!
If you want humbleness,
Be humble with others!
You must decide
what you want from the
Universe!

Acceptance

"I saw souls rejecting me.
Maybe I will see souls disliking me.
But how can I stop loving 'me'?
As God has accepted me.
The way He has created me! "

Creation

God has created each
individual in his unique way
we have not asked Him to create us
this way or that way
we should not waste our time thinking
about the rejections,
"*what others have and we do not have*"
we must accept ourselves happily
and proudly the way we are born.
acceptance of ourselves
brings that confidence
which leads us to new horizons.

trust your heart trust your instinct,
if you feel a difference in your
thoughts
and actions
then you can understand
by yourself
you will not need
any mortal help
you will be the sole survivor,
confidence will grow
more to achieve
the unleashed dreams.

Feel

Do what you feel!

Feel what you do!

Once

i asked the leaves beside my
window
"how old are you?"
leaf ~ "i don't count, i only live
my life with activities and fun."
me "well, what fun you do?"
leaf ~ "i play in the rain
laugh with the wind
smile at the sun
talk to the birds!"

be like the leaf by not counting your age
but by living each moment from your heart.
the moments when gone will never come
back
again in
your life.

Regret

Regret words stay with those people
Who does not wish to turn the pages
Of their book of life.

Persistence

If persistence is the word,
then we all are time travellers
from infancy to kids,
from kids to teens,
teens to adulthood,
to middle age to age
our journey never stops
there was an unknown journey
before we were born
before we came to this earth.
there will be a journey to the
afterlife,
after we leave this world
we are all time travellers
we sail through time
life never stops;
sometimes it just pauses
for a new beginning

hope every soul finds the route
in which their new journey begins.

people who did not have the guts
to follow their heart
they envy you
later when these people see you
with success and happiness,
they will praise you even at your
back.......

Unchanged time

like every sunrise and sunset,
nature, the universe
has fixed everything in their
respective times
you want it to happen now
but it will happen at a specific time.
we cannot change the happenings in
our way
but we are bound to follow its way.

A thing that does not
happen in ten years
suddenly happens in
ten days
miracle keeps on
happening in this
world
the universe
has never broken
the laws of
discipline
for
anyone
for
any
soul.

we all live in this
universe
it feels good that
we are all bound by its
laws equally
no one is above
or beneath
these rules of infinity.
We are all the same
in God's eyes
we all have a
heart
we all possess
feelings
to love and
to appreciate the love
we all have emotions
our look is different
from our perspective
but inside we possess
that tender softness.

- equality

The lift became high.

Wonder when it happened
Wonder how it happened
Nevertheless, it happened in His way!

Positive

A positive mind always earns
a profit in life.
A positive mind is always
hopeful from the inside.
A positive mind always believes
the best things happen
every time.
A positive mind has no
regrets in life.
It never stops seeing the
light.

Exhale

Exhale the negativity.
Exhale the stress out.
Exhale your emotional suffering.
Exhale your pains.
Exhale all these to gain that positivity
from the depth of your heart.
Let there be light again.

The Light

Light appears only after darkness.
your hope is light.
your struggle is light.
your belief in yourself
is the light.
your positivity
is the light.
the light is within
you.
feel it, search it.
it will appear after
the darkness you are struggling
with now.

The Start

It is never too late.
it is never too late for a fresh start
no matter when you start,
at what age or at what time
your choice matters
your wish matters
your happiness behind it matters
it should come from the
core
of your heart.

Stress less

Self-believe develops
when you take a step
ahead to learn
to grow
life is always
to learn
and to grow
stress comes
when you stop giving
your mind something to
feed,
monotonous life gives
stress
feel free to put
your mind
in the place where
you
feel divine.

Despair

when you feel despair
for a longer time
some very big
positive impact is waiting to arrive
you never know what it is
you will only know when
it arrives
when you feel bright from
the inside
and your smile
arrives.

Maintain

The Eight-Letter Word
MAINTAIN

Maintain – Health.
Maintain – Wealth.
Maintain – Family.
Maintain – Relationship.
Maintain – Work.
Maintain – Socialising.
Maintain - Discipline.
Maintain - Happiness.

Tidiness

Be tidy with your wardrobe
Be organised with your work.
Be classy with your presentation.
Be proper with your words.
Be human from your heart.

It is always better to point out the
flaws and mistakes in the person
who is standing inside the mirror.
This will give less complication.

Food for health.
Work for the mind.
Meditation for the soul.
Money to survive.

counting

counting failures
is more valuable
than counting success.
success gives us
satisfaction
success gives us
happiness.
Failures make us strong
makes us
mature
failures develop
our minds
failures raise us to
win and to
survive.

Success
is seductive.
success is satisfaction
with the thought
that you are on
top of the
world.
success also brings tears
to your eyes.
success can be described
as living essences of life
which helps us to breathe
and to endure
our lives,
or may i say
we start breathing
freshly
in a new way.
But why is that?
why are we so happy
about our success?
It only comes after long
days or years of struggling.
we cannot say for
how long

we keep on
wishing,
praying,
working
hard
to satisfy
the satiety value
of our thoughts,
of our souls.
The hardship always
brings fruitful
results,
a mark on our mind
that our hard work
is not gone very
blind.
If we are still alive
with all
our past failures
then we must have
a journey to
reach
our goals,

all those
criticisms,
all those
fail stories
always give meaning
to our lives.
All that helps
us to curve
ourselves
with a strong desire
to be the person
of our dreams.
The journey always
lies between
what we are
and
what we want
to be.
we only have the right
to become
the leading person of
our dream.
"it is always me and
always me."

Unfamiliar
roads
can give you
the vision,
which you have been searching
for a long time,
which familiar roads, does not.
Walking on the familiar road
is easier
it became tough
when the turns arrived
the only thing
we carry with us, is hope
it is only the dream that
keeps us alive,
it's only hope that
keeps us alive,
the inspiration
keeps us moving
it is also the challenges that
keep us pushing.
It is only for the growth
of our mind
by being polite and
by being classy!

"sometimes a smile can do
what words cannot.
wake up every morning
and just smile for you.
you brought it with you.
do not expect your smile
from others only
you have all the right
to smile for being alive
to live every
moment
of your life."

You are the one

The heart is one
God is one.
Love your god first
He has created you.

Love yourself next
as you are his creation.

Love your family because
he has given you
your world of love
and happiness.

Love the world
because it is your home
because he has created
everyone for everyone.

Do not stop

confidence is the key to success
knowledge is the key to confidence
learning is the key to knowledge
being unstoppable is the key to
learning and growth
being unstoppable is the key
to success and happiness.

Just being unstoppable.

SUCCESS

SEARCH

UNIQUE

CATEGORIES

(that) CLEARLY

ENLIGHTEN (YOUR)

SIMPLE SOUL.

Love Speaks

The transparency of a soul
can be seen only by true hearts.

the union

the Universe makes two hearts
unite at the right time!

"Love is not the first time they held
each other
but when they felt for
each other."

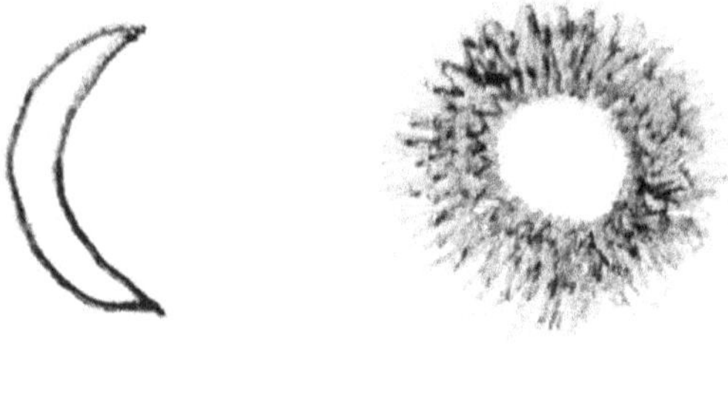

Fall in love

blind people fall in love
deaf people fall in love
weak people fall in love
physically challenged people fall in love
love is a beautiful feeling
it has nothing to do with
what you are
and how you look!

perfection is the word
needed outside your home
in a relationship,
the imperfection words do stay
all the time to make a journey
together
to clear the flaws
together.

"someone who accepts you
with all your
flaws and madness
that person loves
you the most..."

"a true lover falls in love
with all your imperfections
stand always there
besides all your mistakes
to blend it more
beautifully
to make them
cheerfully."

"silence has its language
a truly loving partner understands
the words of silence."

"Love is
that
freeness
which
we
both
need
to bind
us
together."

be a free soul first
to know thyself
then only you can
give the person
you love,
respect!

"before love binds us.
we both need to love ourselves.
let us feel our soul
before we feel us...

"I cannot show you, my love.
I gave the job
to the Universe
to make you only feel my
heart!"

"Love is when you hurt me and you get hurt more!"

"If thinking about me is hurting you,
then you are in love with me the most!"

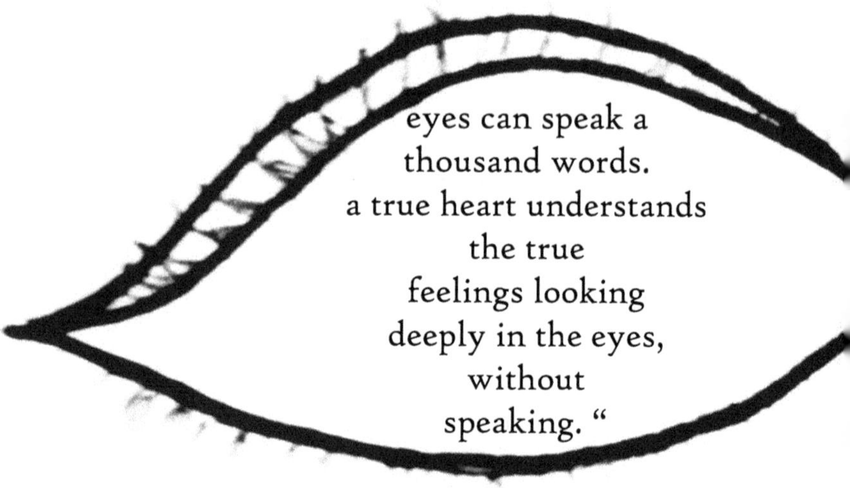

eyes can speak a
thousand words.
a true heart understands
the true
feelings looking
deeply in the eyes,
without
speaking. “

love

looks do not describe love
but eyes do
style does not describe love
but simplicity does
the body does not describe love
but feel does
love is eternal, love is the soul
love is clarity, love is a smile
love means the world,
love means the mind,
love is a feeling,
love is the binding,
love is the passion
behind every vision
love is complete
when you are mine.

"when you see the face
you cannot feel love
when you feel love
the real beauty of the
face is revealed."

trust is like a tree, which needs
many years to grow
and
needs very few moments
to cut
to break
the heart

“beauty is not something
to express with dresses
and makeup
the best part of it is
unseen by the
eyes.”

"search for the beautiful soul
beauty lies in the words
beauty lies in the manner
beauty lies in every part
other than the body and looks
a frame cannot capture the
real beauty
of a true
soul"

"you do not have to show
your beauty to others
the beauty will be seen
and cherish
by the right person
then it will become
timeless.

“LOVE HIM LIKE ANYTHING IN
THE WORLD
BUT LOVE YOURSELF LIKE YOU
ARE THE WORLD.”

<u>a small reminder</u>

"beneath her body
lies her soul
look at her closely
she lives inside
that body
love her the way
she is
do not design her
for your greed
you will get burned on
time indeed."

"Love is the intimacy of two souls!
thus it is said –
a soul mate."

Pour the relationship of water
into the bowl of respect
let it stand,

to face the heat of the sun
and cold of the moon.

Nature Heals

Open sky

have you seen the open sky?
i do not know why you feel shy
look at the open space;
look at the airy place
it all makes you feel how tiny you are
it all makes you feel how loving you
are
look at the birds
they are flying in the sky
look at the strength
they are getting from the sky
the birds are tinier in comparison to
us
they are stronger but stronger than us,
they have wings that can touch the
sky
we are the admirers
to see how beautifully they
fly!

love becomes you

"love becomes you when you fall
in love with you
love becomes you when you break
the boundaries
within you
your love for yourself will let you fall
in love with life
let your journey on earth be
blossom and bright."

earth

the exotic corners of the earth
are calling me
they are calling me to feel
my presence on earth
in a new way
to fall in love
to feel the girl of that
heaven
not with the looks and
not with the
styles,
we are the guests of fair
designs
we cannot be in more than
one place at a time
so cherish the moments
in a way to
bind.

rainbow

have you noticed the rainbow?
how beautifully curved
have you noticed the stars?
why always twinkling at us
have you seen the green pastures?
like a carpet on the land
have you noticed the mountain peak?
how tallest they stand
do you ever wonder?
why they are here?
Like a friend to us
to live with us and to cheer.

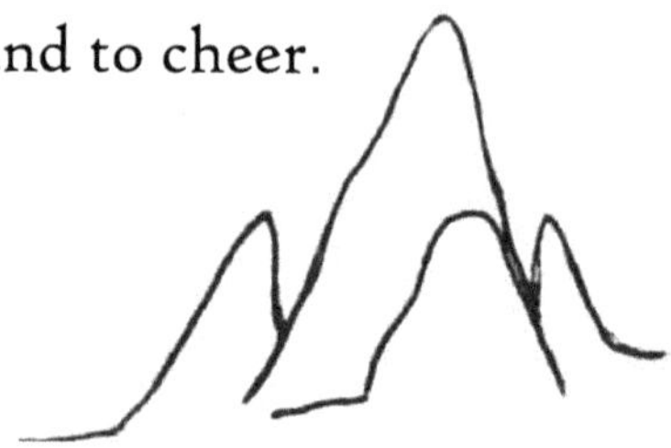

my smile

"you cannot take away my smile
i smile from the heart
you cannot control my heart
my heart is controlled by my soul
and my soul is connected
to the universe!

i want to be air

i want to be air to fly high and low
i want to be air with no attachment to
grow
i want to be air to travel and to move
i want to be air to develop my mood.

want to listen to the
whispers of the trees
want to swim with
dolphins and fish
want to travel the mountain's tip
want to know what they storing deep.

i want to fly with the clouds and birds
i want to see the dawn and the dusk
to see to feel every corner of the earth
i want to be air and
i want to be air!

you

you are one soul who is greeted by
the sun
you are one soul who is greeted by
stars
you are one soul who came to live
in the world.
to be you is a pleasant journey
within the journeys of all
so feel it and start it you can make
it your way............

you can make it happen for you
and for you,

you can live a million ways.

Self-worth

not same

you are not
the same person anymore
you are not the same person
when you were young,
you are not the same person,
when you enjoyed your first date,
you are not the same person
who had a crush on someone,

you are not the same person
who had experienced the
first breakup,
you are not the same person
who experienced betrayal
even though your loyalty was there,
you are not the same person
who has lost your dear ones,

the transformation occurs
after every chapter, you cross.

the formation
keeps on occurring
to make you grow

like a caterpillar to a butterfly

it makes you grow mentally
to make you learn more about life,

- *you are maturing*

life has transformed you
time has changed you
you are much stronger
then the person you were,
change happens and it keeps on
happening
whether you like it or not
life keeps on changing,
you have to grow despite all the
troubles
that keeps coming.
As a human,
you must travel through the
suffering.
One day will come when you
will thank
for all your pains
which transforms you in such a
way that
you can now blend yourself with
the unbound happiness.

time

time, which does not wait for anyone
carries all the
answers
past is known
the future is unknown
the unknown future stores
bring all the answers
to both asked and unasked questions,
the past time improves us
makes us stronger for the coming
lifespan
time only follows
it's timetable
without breaking
its own rules and discipline.

mistake

mistakes happen in our life
not in our way
but in
God's way
he creates it to show us the
right path
mistakes are a one-time
reading book
repeating any mistake
is the real mistake one
makes.

One cannot pass through the barrier
one made for themselves
be your guide
to open up
the entire barrier
of your mind.

a happy soul

be a happy soul
you are not bound by
laws and rules
you came alone and
you will travel back
alone,
let yourself flow
with time
with all the faith in you;
see the beauty
of
every moment
of life.

create your own sphere where you wish to stay. no matter anyone comes new in your life or anyone goes out, if anyone cuts you deep and the wound refuses to heal. you must come back in that very world of your own where you feel safe with your feelings and where you believe you live. born again from there like a fresh new-born. absorb the energy of light to heal that broken part and move on.

after that long time pause of
silence
now you found all the
answers
you were searching
for
now you want that
part to heal you from
the inside.
thus, your journey
has just begun,
to fall in love
with yourself
the most among
all the other things
in the world.

- *become rich*

you have gained the courage
to fight with fear.
you learned
the most important challenge
is to accept
everything
that has life
given.

- *allow yourself*

to fill your heart with the warmth of
greatness
in the absence of
anxiety
to be humble with
yourself and with
others
to forgive those who
wounded you,
so that you do not need to
carry
the wound in the
future.

- *release*

the real you

you are now feeling
the presence of your soul
like never before
now you know the happiness
lives inside

explore your mind
the way it takes you.

you learn the presence
of darkness in life,
which helps to learn
the importance of light,
now you understand
the faith that you are born with
the faith that is the only saviour
you will carry;
to be in a positive light
and to be in merry,
the faith you bring with
you
will always guide you
to take the next steps
towards life.
Faith is the universe
and the faith is you.

- *keep believing*

Prepare yourself
for coming tomorrow,
with your prayers
and faith in you.
No need to say
the coming time is
unknown,
while your prayers
will be known
by the infinity
and
by your soul.

Your clarity is not for everyone
you met or confide in
it is for your inner self.
not everyone understands you,
as they cannot.
It is your job only to
understand yourself.
Not everyone can feel the way
you feel for your heart.
You can be underestimated by many.

But there are and there will be many
Who will appreciate your thoughts and
mind
when you put it
in some powerful actions in your life.
When your work will become
your passion,
your gesture can earn criticism
and leave you in hurdles.

But your passion for life will make
you exist within them and
make you live in a
gracefully.

You are the one
who can kill it,
kill it from the inside.
The pain,
the frustration
that is blocking
your path
towards your
happiness
you can make your
move
to end it first
before it eats
you like a
monster.

Be alone
for yourself,
just be
with you.
take a deep dive
into your heart and
know your purpose
to be here on earth.

you are here
to live to cherish your life
with that beautiful
gift that you brought
with you
within your inner
self.

No one can take your
place the way you can.
No one can stop you if
you do not stop yourself.
You are a soul who came
into this world to live
to make your
place,
the Universe has created
you
and it did not leave
you alone,
you have to know
that
believe that
from your heart
then only you can
prove your
worth
to yourself
first!

you are surviving every moment;
you are surviving the odd,
the reckless, and
the prejudices,
you are not leaving
not running away
from the
situation.
you are brave to struggle alone
in every
circumstance
you are a creator's creation
of *magic and norm*
you do not know
what power do you possess
inside,
you are not responsible
for your power
the power belongs to the universe
who is your Creator.

Not any soul came empty-handed
in this world
every soul is unique with its
nature, skills,
kindness, and greatness.
there should not be any comparison
with others because what others
have you do not have,
and what you have the universe has
provided you with a gift
as your identity.
Exploring your mind will let you
discover yourself and
your skills.
The universe is not harsh on
you when you have faith
inside your heart,
when you know that
the supreme power
is kind to every soul
on earth.

HE *CREATED YOU,*
YOU BECOME ***HIS***
OBEDIENT
AND
HE *SHOWERS*
HIS *BLESSINGS*
ON YOU TO
ENLIGHTEN YOUR
SOUL.

When something bad happens
that tore us apart
it becomes a heavy burden on our
hearts,
we can feel the ocean of deep
wounds inside
but are unable to show anyone
outside,
smiles lost from our
mind.

With every passing time,
that wound stays in us
searching for an answer
to why this
terrible thing had
happened.

The purity of our hearts keeps
searching
until that one day,
that **purity** finds the
answer,

we understand that
the pain was worth it,
that wound has left
the mark of
sustenance.
That wound is
completing us from
the inside,
that wound makes us feel
the reality of our
life
we can now see
things more
clearly.

- observe

Now move forward
with that survival
strategy,
that pain becomes the actual
gain
of our life.
The ache
that could not destroy
you
gives you a new
pair of wings
to elevate your
life.

When a soul is receiving true love
it is receiving
the value of its
presence
a presence that
enlightens to give
away
that life which was
unpolished,
uncared,
and
uncultivated,
never received that
feeling
which can transform the
soul to heal
from the
wound
that was a burden through
the years.

The love goes deep
digging inside
to make you realise
the essence of your being
and you feel the world
alive.

We all have feelings
we all have emotions
we all need love
we all need affection.
We all need care
we all need to feel special.

We expect better from
everyone
We expect kindness from
others
We want ourselves to
bind
only with pure
love,
only with
happiness,
with
gentleness.

We are all same
when it comes to the
matter of the
heart.
Humbleness;
humanity
matters to all of us.
Then also we fight,
we see the
difference
in respect of
colour, looks,
rich, poor,
love, and hate.
In the end, we all
remain human,
came only with a soul
inside to live in this
beautiful home
called Mother Earth.
yes, we are the **world.**

Birth

Birth

She is the power of
the way she was born.

But when she looks at her through
other's eyes;
She is naive in her body and mind.

She is the power, the way she
thinks but when she looks and is
compared to other's minds she
finds herself
in no place to land.

When she finds her eyes in the
mirror and no one is looking at her,
she thinks in her mind, who is she
when she arrives in this world
wearing her skin?

She thought wasn't herself enough
to fight on with a negative mind.

She gives herself a push that she
must rise.
Whatever it is or whoever it is, she
must listen
to the word
her mind speaks.
And she must follow what
her heart feels.

She is the one among the galaxies
of the universe.
Like it shines in the darkness and
makes its presence known to other
parts.
She is the birth of her birth as she
carries all the elements
which are among the
stardust.

She will be shining high when she
feels the sky is her roof and the
ground is her way towards her
home.
She is on her own when she carries
all her thoughts into
action.

She ignored who said, "What are
you?

And she ignored who said, "Grab a
man's hand to become stable and to
become someone's
wife.

You know you are a girl who needs
support to stay and gather the
wealth of pleasure and happiness
which will make you happier
in this world.

She refused to understand
'support' from any other
hand.
She makes way just closing the
door of the world, which never tells
you you are the master
of your happiness and
you are your world
of your own.

The world only loves people with
fame,
But she wonders what is 'fame' she
will know herself!

She is transforming,
forming,
becoming.
With every wound
erase a part of her skin.
With every criticism,
she has bravely taken.
With every disrespect
she received.
She only chose to move on
with her honesty and courage.
For she believes in her
God so much,
nothing could break her knees.

And that’s where it all began.
Her mother knew that she would be born as a girl.
She heard it when she grew up.
She wonders in her mind, what makes her mother know that she will be a girl child.

That gives her the thought about the power which exists in the world.
That someone up there is constantly hearing us,
watching us,
seeing us.
if I speak in my mind it's never going to be washed away in between the stars.

She learned this first lesson from her mom, that when you remain true to yourself the power stays inside your heart.

And the search began.

She searched among the clouds to catch a glimpse of that power.

She searched among the grass to see a light arise in a part.

She searched among the trees to see if it was lying somewhere among the branches.

Her eyes keep on rotating to know that power which never fades away once it can be seen.

Suddenly she reminds herself

My mother hasn't seen that power ever
then how come she speaks in her mind

Does that mean the power lives inside
our hearts?

The question became the answer

And the answer became the question.

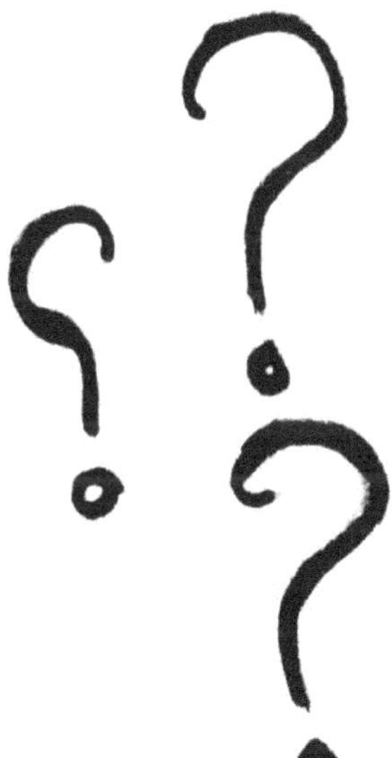

Where am I searching if it has a connection with our beliefs?

- "The connection became the bond that the beginning kept on talking to me whenever I found the world needed a hearing aid for my thoughts"!

I appreciate myself for everything I have.

- ***all is a gift***

With time spent I grow.

Learned the world more around me.

And through the box where people of different shapes and sizes and words keep entertaining.

There I saw the world of people of a different kind.

"I learned it's not only the world I see around is mine".

There is a world outside this world and
I am a part of it too.

- English has taught me to grow and become a part of this globalisation.

(programs of The USA and UK,
through the network of Bangladesh)

Television

I fall in love with what I see.

Somewhere seems I belong to thee.

The roads, the dresses, the houses, the interior seem like mine somewhere.

I loved the way they speak, they walk

As if I know them as if like I was there...

- in past life (maybe)

With what magic it occurred as it rests in my heart always like my home.

- dreamt of being there one day soon.

I started to learn English as my mother wanted.

- English medium school

My mother gave me a world of my own

where music

art

dance stayed.

It is as if I was born in more than one world.

- journey of childhood

I grew and my dreams grew with me.

No one knew and nobody asked where I
wanted to go and where my dreams
would make the curve

- journey to the dream.

when a child is born on earth.

We don't see her as a soul on earth rather we began to decorate her body and pure mind in the way we want to.

We are pure from our mind to give this new-born all love and blessings but unable to help her, the new-born to cherish her mind the way she appears on earth;

to be a new human with new thoughts and new creations.

We judge without the need to know what her belongings are. We need to make arrangements for her growth without understanding that she has a developed mind to be on her chosen path of her own.

To be unable to know the newborn soul as she grows and expands with her mind we began to flourish our thoughts in her brain.

The birth always brings new fortune but we begin to judge everything in our way.

Maybe we are afraid to know the new-born thoughts she brought with her.

> *Let her grow as she grows independently with her ability to expand her mind.*

Where to find and where to begin the journey of my dream?

I was enjoying every bit of life that I was learning.....

Childhood was tough

Not to mention why

I was growing but without the happy word written on all my pages of life.

My love for my parents was strong but when it comes to taking I always found half is complete and half remains vacant.

Can't understand why is that.

But now I can say it was that...

- mom remains everything in my life.

She became my sky
She became my dream of every night
She was there even in the storm
She has never ruined my home.
She gave me a home with courage being
the wall and honesty being the roof
- guided me in all the
moments

She told me "Make your own home.

no matter how hard but you shall never give up."

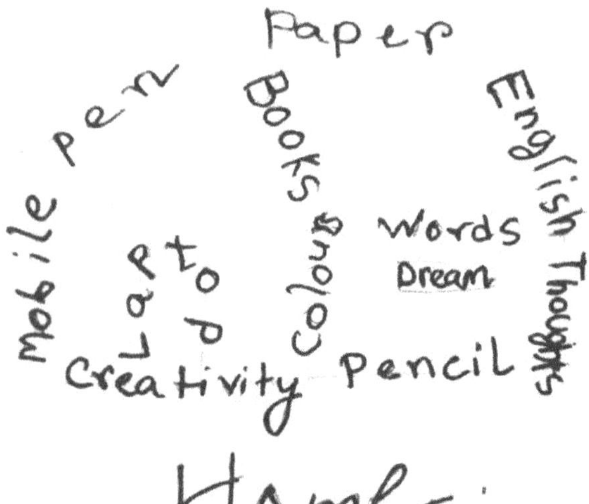

Every storm arose between the walls she
looked at me and said you are special
and you are my only treasure.

- she never gave up

Her dream was to see my life only with happiness around.

Who to blame and whom to say the question stays always?.....

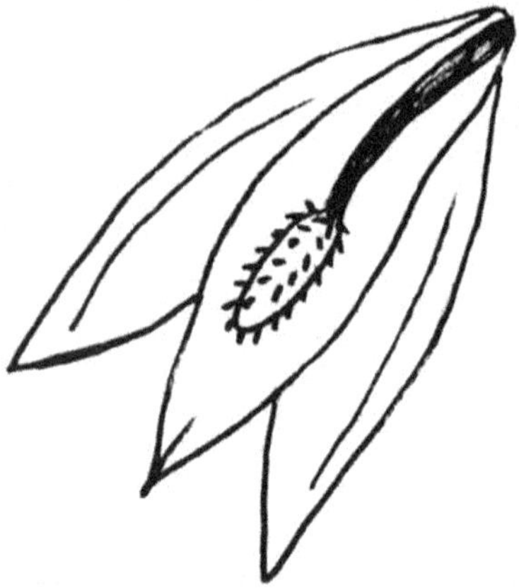

I grew up in a house made of brittle walls. So my mind was grown strong.

So when I look back anytime,
think of the coming struggle.

I see the journey has given my roots the water of capability and the sunlight of ability.

- The never give up mentality.

With faith in me like my mother who
knew she would have a daughter

I too know that one day I will be living
my dreams..

days passed as I graduated,

my journey

the outer home was fascinating.

My old days always haunt me so I looked forward to building a new home for me and my mom where no wrong hands will ever touch our bones and I will never scream.

- Something I do not mention to the outer world; only my neighbours know.

Life was not so painful when I explained my childhood but life wasn't natural. I was born to a happy family being the only child of my parents but everything wasn't right from the beginning there was homely violence my mom has faced all her life. I grew up looking at the abnormal things most of the nights.

Drinks and smokes
are not that bad
when compare to
the mentality of a
brutal heart.

I believed in kindness as

I was showered with love

by every sibling of

my mother and

their father and

their mother

- my maternal
  parents

Compassion

Kindness

Empathy

I learned them from

my mama bari!

- (maternal uncle is known as mama and the whole of the maternal side, we call in Bengali 'mama bari')

How could I ever lose sight of them
who blessed me only with proper
care and gentleness?

- i ran there every
evening and morning
for there was no fear.

I love them and they remind me every day.

Whenever I found the heaviness in my brain I searched for all my dadu and dida and mama around.

- Searching for a safe place.

At times I know like that they have a
soft heart inside and outside, the same

- They never became
my strength.

The world is round

Whenever I run from the weakness in me it comes to me around.

I began to search for a place of work from where I could start to see my dream.

I changed job after job but nothing changed in me except the heart falls for someone.

As in the teens I have a full right to fall in love with the person with whom I can mend.

When I thought everything would fall
into place

career, marriage and the rest.

Time has its own story to tell....

Success didn't come from any place.

Nor that I was shattered but I grew with a strong mind that one day, I will remember these days.

- Smilingly

I was always positive inside and outside
for there I believed in myself...

I learned every moment that
whatever is happening if it's not
my plan then it is someone's plan
- I believed always

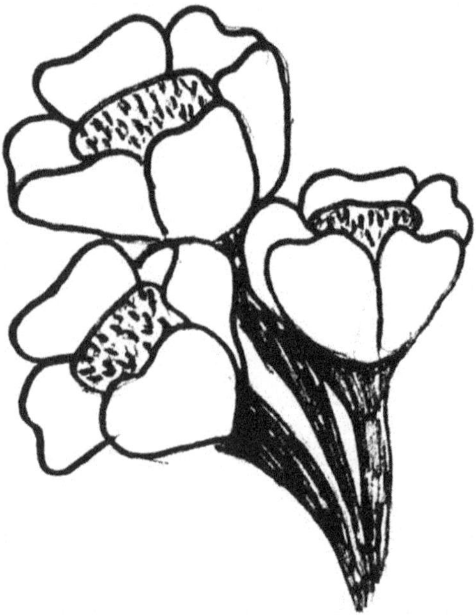

My choice has no choice I follow the time the way it came and the way it mends

I do know that every moment I am enjoying is the moment.

With friends and family and a push to become a lady in the row, I was growing both mentally and soulful way.

I never welcomed disappointment in my life

My belief was always strong about my life.

I acknowledge the acquaintances and the ignorance together

for they meant to help to learn about the world which is made of both bad and good.

I didn't feel sorrow as I was in a learning manner.

I lived the moments fully for I knew if it's gone would never face my life again.

When you find my friend whether you are a girl of teenage time or a boy who wants to become a gent,

I tell you to live the moments truthfully for they will leave you with wisdom and knowledge to grow.

You will receive the messages that are gathering in your heart

In future, it will help in self guard.

I learned not to turn the table when it is all set.

So I didn't judge anyone who came and said a hi and a bye onset.

You are emerging within those moments you are facing and will never regret the past in your heart saying, "Oh, I never enjoyed those days which were telling me to fly in the true-false sky.

I loved each moment when they
became a part of my life

And still never regret those failures
and sorrows.

I never gave up trying every road I
was taking but let me tell you not a
single road I found helping.

I hadn't met success ever but I knew
that it was standing impending.

That belief has stayed in me even
when I fall.

I awaken every morning just like any
other day and at night I go to bed to
wake for the other morning.

The days went by with a long period
of silence like I hadn't met the road
where my attainment.

Sometimes I looked outside the
window and looked at the sky as if
I met a very close friend of mine.

Years passed like this way and I shattered one day while travelling a road that I thought was mine.

I came home.

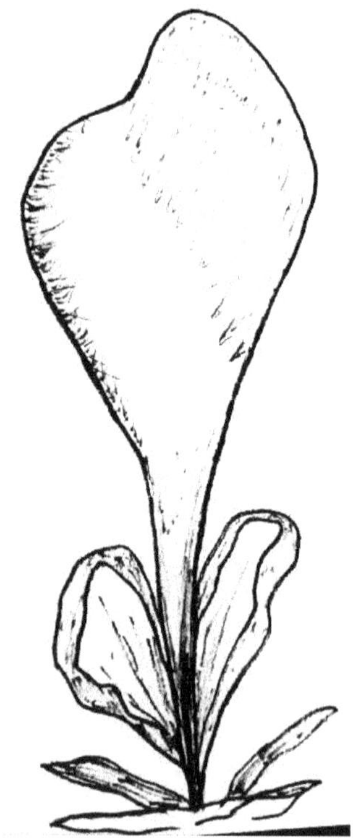

The pain has killed the girl who used to exist and keeps smiling even on the avalanches.

That girl is no longer alive in this world

As she was killed not by any heart she trusted

She was killed by trusting the wrong who she thought was human.

I apologised to myself every time I felt the pain inside which was taking me to rise in a new way.

How can I forgive myself for trusting the wrong hand?

I kept weeping for several days, months and years.

I apologise to my God for not
understanding the bad world outside.

But then I found the answer in me

That how could I learn the bad if
haven't faced it myself?

Everything became clear in my head,
it was the road that was making me
not breaking me.

It was the path I needed to travel
before I grew as a fighter of strong
sense and wisdom.

I chose it because I wanted to learn the
difference between worst and
wholesome.

I wanted to travel the curses before I
got my bliss.

It is that my journey hasn't ended it
has a new beginning.

Every road has landed me in the
awareness of becoming right.

I chose me after that *every time*.

I have chosen my heart.

That falls every night for pure love,
who else can love me the way I can?

I chose the answers that helped me to
regain myself.

- I was growing
  I was healing.

Healing is not the power you need
from others when you choose yourself
first then you become your answers.

- Healed by myself

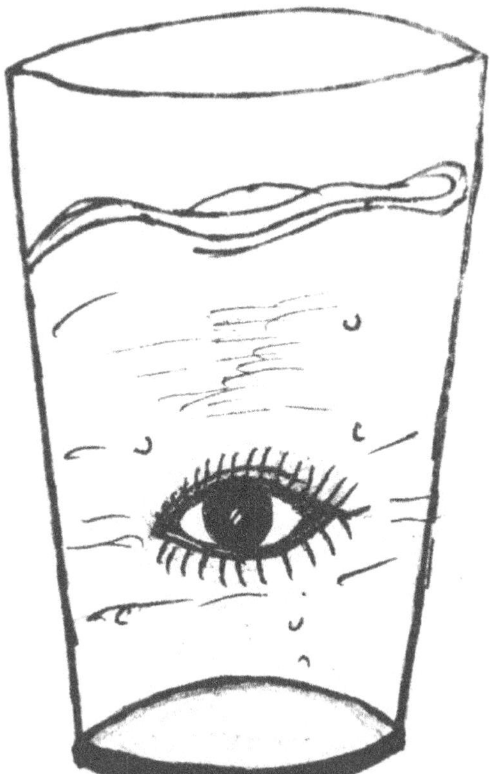

I first noticed the words were coming into my mind when I was doing nothing. I wanted to write them just like I used to write in classes for my friends on their birthdays.

Making cards and decorating them with lovely words that instantly evolved in my heart.

And lastly, I filled it with colours and pieces I drew myself.

Lovely it looked to me and they appreciated it.

- Never thought I could have the ability to write and decorate those words with sketches and colours.

I felt the real me when I held the pen
in my grip
in my
hand.

Nothing could stop me from
expressing my soul.

As my soul is the only power that
helps me soar.

The soul is the real you. You are the one who is captivated inside this body. No one can touch your soul. No one can see the real you if they do not have a pure heart. No one can deny you if you do not deny yourself from falling. You are your power when you get that feeling somewhere from deep inside. You can lead you to walk on your chosen road. You are your home when you find that peace deep down your throat. You are kind to yourself that is the reason you can hear the voices that are emerging in you. And you are caring that words are telling you to do what next. You are humble when you respect your soul as the only gift you hold. Your soul cannot break and thus cannot grow. Your soul is the most powerful of anything in the world. No one can capture and bind your soul. It will stay inside you and will remain yours forever.

Stay there.

Stay there where you feel you grow.

You are appreciated.

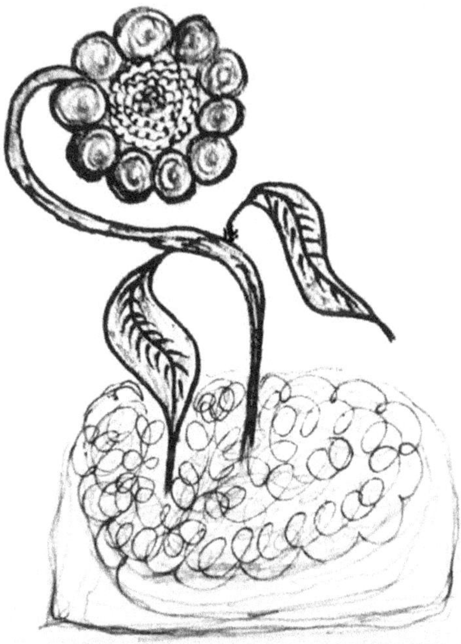

Marriage is the word dedicated to the world of girls like they are a marriageable product.

No one asks," How are you and what is your goal.

People see them only as a nuptial bulb.

I disagreed with the close ones and the ones who say

When are you bonding with the person and how is he?

What type of society we have grown up in where there is no place for a girl alone?

The girl who was loved and pampered for so many years

Only, considered a decorative part.

She has the right to live her life the way she wants. Why don't you understand and why don't you learn?

She is not a product of your satire.

She is a girl of flesh and sapphire.

You are connecting her with someone whom she hasn't chosen.

And you say as if she is your purpose of living though she hasn't had the right to choose her own.

You called her and told her to get married.

Isn't marriage a personal belonging of two souls with their choices and rights to choose?

You say you are her wellwishers

Well, what wish do you do for her when you cannot ask her what her wish is?

No one can deny the fact that she is a human.

But where are you standing when you find her in a desperate situation?

You are born not to submerge someone's mind.

You are born to live and let live other's vibes.

Believe her happiness in which she believes.

Answer her question which is arising in her mind.

When you cannot heal her wounds
which are bleeding from her soul.

Then you have no right to put her in a
place of yours.

You are emerging from the duty to put
her in a pot she doesn't know and you
put her in a place which she hasn't
chosen alone.

Leave her alone if she wants to be.

Leave her and give her the freedom to
feel the earth belongs to her.

If you cannot become hers then at
least you do not snatch
her from her.

She has no one in her life.

But she has chosen *herself* from the
first cry.

You cannot deny the fact that she is
not unhappy.

She learned from her life that before
getting married to someone she first
married her mind. what her mind
wants and what helps her to smile.

She is not alone,
she has her soul to answer all her
queries and all her demands on time.

She has chosen her mind for her before
she binds with someone else for the
rest of her life.

She has learned from her true self that
if she cannot become happy with
herself, there is no one whom she can
blame.

And she has stopped blaming others
for her happiness.

You chose her
as a decorative piece
for your written book
but she was born with the mind
to write her book.

never neglect her words
she is a born writer
of positive vibes and
she allowed herself to spread
those vibes...

- becoming a writer
is not her choice
it is her birthright
that flows from her
soul and
her mind.

The strength lies

In acceptance.

Her mind is strong as she has accepted
her
despite her flaws.

I belong to the ocean of thoughts

She said.

I belong to the world of words.

She whispered.

I belong to the world of creation.

She mentions.

She held a pen in her hand and
allowed it to flow.

She held the colours in her brush and
allowed the mind to become her guide
with every stroke she made.

She is evolving when she closes the
door to the outside world.

She stays alone whispering the
thoughts that are echoing inside her.

She allows her.

And she grows.

Free yourself

from the

false

bindings.

Inherited

from your

soul.

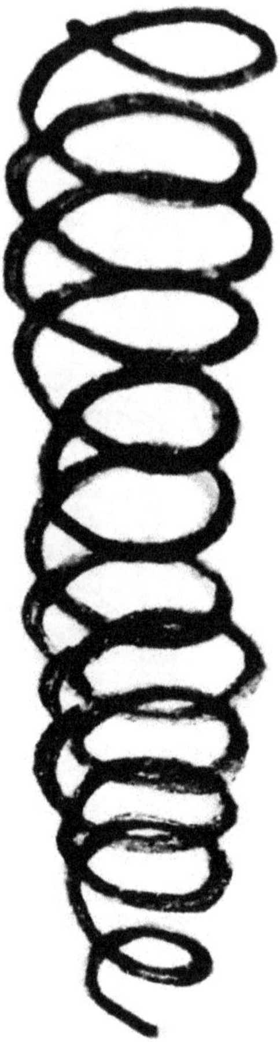

Soar

Your wings were never clipped.
Just it has never spoken to you.

Let it go.
It means
its time
to fly
above
the
wind.

- Wind which
  heavily
  filled
  her
  lungs

When you realise your wings
your extension mind,
trust me
you will
start to
feel the
pain
mild
and
faded.

Search your imperfections.
they exist.
which you have neglected
for all these
years
speaks
about the attachment
you have
to it.

Listen to your heart.

It beats.

What is *poetry* to you?

The answer came:

My heart says;

When it comes to love
stop chasing it
let it come.

When it comes to desire
Allow your breath to hold the fire.

When it comes to marriage
Wait until you feel the other half of
your life.

When it comes to giving birth
Only choose the purity of air and your
heart.

When it comes to speaking about life.
you must choose to smile.
Because every truthful journey ends
with a smile.

When it comes to finding
the meaning of life
Pause for a moment
And say
Life is a journey
Of both
Darkness
And
Light.

You need
to hammer
the darkness
to bring
the light

The journey is long
do not try to cut off
each moment
is necessary
for
the growth
of mind
and
soul.

Your journey matters.
Your wish matters.
Your life matters.
Your voice for yourself matters.
You are a soul.
Your presence matters.

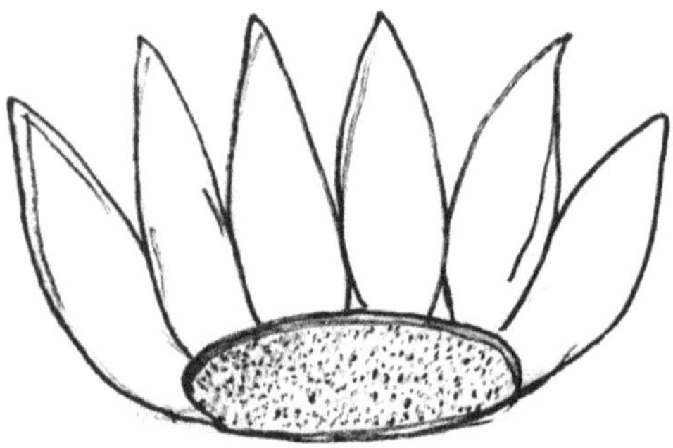

Do not give up.
Do not go against your heart.
Do not concise your dreams.
Do not suppress your gifts.

Set yourself free
not to harm any
soul.
But to feel your
soul.

Give yourself all the time
it needs.

making

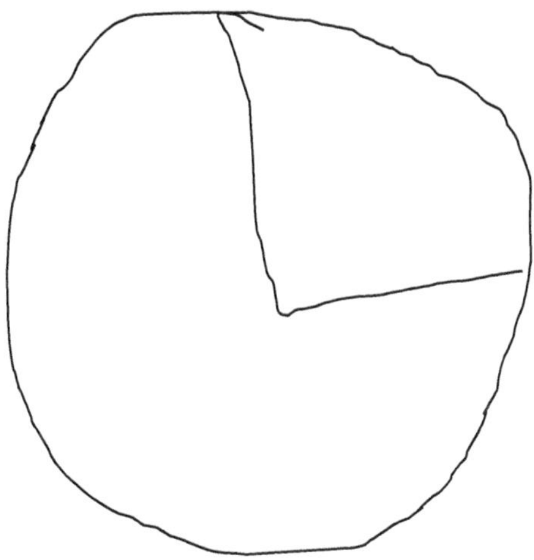

evolution

growth

Before healing starts.
Believe you will be healed.

There is a garden in your heart.
which needs your sunlight smile
and fertile soil of hope.
You are the only gardener
God has appointed for you.
So, you must care about the
flowers
that bloom.
You keep pouring the smile and
the water of grace.
Let it stand sweetly
as the smile
on your face.

What does hope do?
It creates a path for you to walk.
It leads the weak to harden.
It gives the best wishes all the
time.
It prepares you to leap up to your
thoughts of mind.
It reacts to the world of sorrow.
You must not stay there
where hope dies.
You must change your path when
it comes to belief in life.
One must chase the light.

Thank you to all
who broke me.
Thank you to all
who tore me.
Thank you to all
who betrayed me.
and

Thank you to all
who have never
left my site
I thank my Universe
for giving me
a life
like this
which has curved me
to become
Me
today.

You are special
when you believe.
You are special
when you feel.
You are awesome
when you care.
You are worthy
when you become.

Every formation has a new story.
Every new creation has a new
beginning.
Every hope gives you a lift.
Every lift makes you rise.
Thus my first
written birth
I present
to you
A lift In life.

My Little Words

Pleasant

life has taken an unwanted field
life can be parametric staff
you care about your move
you are a bundle of hope.
no one would believe much
how do you achieve the fun?
you are the survivor of past and
present
you can be a various way to make
yourself pleasant.

Agony

once upon a time
i travelled to find my agony
i was unaware of how things
make me possessed of love and merry.
you might find curiosity about life
exists
you knew the fall of rising to renew
you can suffer them howsoever
you are a performer on a stage ever.

Saviour

who might consider the practical
affair?
i consider the very best failure
where i gave the presence of the Saviour
and i guess that achieves my founder
of the protective career.

Ability

they see your inability
you search and find your ability,
they see your mistakes and flaws
those are only your stairs of growth,
they hold fear in their eyes
you fight with it every day
to shine more brightly,
for they are not people to praise
while you live in this body
whom you must raise and praise.

\- *everyday*

A Few Answers

what is life?
life is a mystery.

what is love?
a blessing from God.

what is a smile?
your existence profile.

what is suffering?
helping you to climb the stairs of life.

what is a dream?
work.

do you believe in god?
my existence is the word.

Who are you
ask yourself
the day you find the answer
journey begins!

Author's words

people only find my inability
i keep searching and proving
to myself my ability,

they consumed what they think
i prove that i am a happy soul
and
i must live,

life is a pleasure
i must be aware of that feeling
i must not be aware of what
others think of my guts and my
cheering,

i care about my love for myself
and why should i care about
what others have

i love myself the most in this
world and i must conceive that.

i let them live only with their
despair,
i control my feelings towards
the people who have this
negative affair

i love myself looking at a new
horizon with ever-new dreams
i love myself for what i have and
what i can give.

sometimes

Sometimes we need to free ourselves
from everything that is going on in our
mind
the present time is teaching us to
become
the person for our future,

but thinking too much about
our family, our work, or us
we sometimes forget about the person
we are;

all our wishes vanish from our mind
we forget about the dreams we were
chasing
we forget about the roads that we started
creating
confusion occurs;
we give up on what we can give
our power diminished,

That is the very time when we need to
bring ourselves
to the centre of our mind
from where our thoughts begin
from where we can see the world
the way we want to see it.

We need to bring ourselves back
before everything becomes a stranger to
us,
even we need to find ourselves from time
to time.

I believe this happens with every human
being
when sometimes they cannot recognise
the person they are.

Holding everything in your heart
let us bring back by simply giving us
some special time to ourselves
showing our heart that
yes, we care about you,
your existence and your love.

I am successful

if i can change an unhappy soul
to a happy soul.
if i can bring a smile to any face
who cannot smile on his own
if people read my words for
inspiration and motivation
i am successful.

i am successful when i can change that
teardrop into a
smile
before it touches the lips.
i am successful when i bring some love
and kindness
to any heart which is affected by any
harshness.

i am successful when i can bring hope to
any soul.
if you like my words then i am
successful.
my success is not limited to fame and
money.

i want to live in **hearts** and stay there.
i am a happy soul
and i am successful.

finish

mirror mirror on the wall,
tell me where the
beautiful hearts live
in this world.

i wish i could meet them
i wish i could admire them
tell them how beautifully
special they are.
i wish i could spend
my time with them.

wish people all of
a beautiful mind
so there won't be
any broken hearts
living here to die.

About the Author.

Jinia M.

A poetess, a novel writer, and a painter put all her thoughts and skills into writing books. Her first published book 'A Lift In Life' came out as a lift in her life. She never thought of becoming an Author. But it has flown out from her heart as if everything was pre-decorated and embedded in her soul. In the year 2015, she met with an accident that destroyed her physical strength but she rose only by practising yoga for one and a half years. She wanted to start a career as a content writer. But her subconscious mind landed her to be an author. She was naive with her mind when she thought of writing something to share with the world. But her self-love and self-compassion were the only strength to embark on the journey. She wrote her first book in 2019 but started self-publishing by reprinting her first and second book in 2021. She is the author of two books; prose and poetry.
Born and brought up in Kolkata, India. She doesn't represent her country, culture or religion. She is only a soul when it comes to writing and painting thus; writes her name as Jinia M. Her full name is Jinia Mondal.

Acknowledgement

To my mother.

Who was everything to me when I was little. She gave me a world of my own. I cannot become anything without her guidance, her knowledge, and her enthusiasm. She gave me birth but she has given my mind to be born like me with always a courageous and honest push. She can take the mountain down for me and she is the one who could always help me to create my own home on a mountain peak. Everything I am today is only because of her. She is my mother of dignity and mental strength. I adore her for whatever she has given me.

About the book

This book carries all the positive side that flows within me. This book contains my life journey, which has made me who I am today. This is a helping hand to think deeply about the next move when you are in hard situations. There are answers given about the reason behind the trauma, stress, and failures. A book for a lift to rise. I am wishing and sending you that 'aura and hope' which will tell you to rise for a better tomorrow. Whatever the situation the words can become the answers to many complexities. May you find yourself connected with that higher essence that resides inside you and everywhere.

My social accounts.

Instagram @ **wordsinpen**

Facebook @ **wordsinpen**

Twitter @ **Jinia_Mondal**

Website: **www.jiniamondal.com**

www.ingramcontent.com/pod-product-compliance
Ingram Content Group UK Ltd.
Pitfield, Milton Keynes, MK11 3LW, UK
UKHW020051200726
13845UKWH00056B/777

9 789354 262050